PQRS a poets theater script
by Patrick Durgin

Chicago: Kenning Editions

PQRS

Cover art by Julietta Cheung: "*PTBT* (2000–3) is a series of color photographs that depicts various kinds of processed raw meats in the guise of the nature photography genre. I am interested in the becoming image of the dematerialized bodies. As photography multiplies singular images, this deterritorializing effect became the basis of my material investigation—a reversal of the distributive impact by transfiguring details and fragments into image."

Cover design by Jeff Clark / Quemadura

Interior composition by Patrick Durgin

Printed on recycled paper

PQRS: A Poets Theater Script
ISBN: 978-0-9846475-7-6 $12.95

Published by Kenning Editions
www.kenningeditions.com
© 2013 by Kenning Editions for Patrick Durgin

Distributed to individuals and the trade by
Small Press Distribution
1341 Seventh Street
Berkeley, CA 94710-1409
1-800-869-7553
www.spdbooks.org

Act One: Scene One

Music begins—an indifferent drone on a viola or similar instrument. Not lugubrious but curling gradually and precisely around a certain pitch. It matters that the lighting compliments the performance space rather than framing an illusion within it. Also that no "color" be used, only different chromatic qualities of light, just to oppose darkness. Not just cans and gels, but different types of light fixtures, various sources.

Light falls on S who is in the center of the stage, huddled over, head down, i.e. "child's pose." She faces away from us. S wears a dress that is loose, simple, indefinite and neutral. The pace of her move-ments, as with the delivery of her lines, is slow and deliberate. She speaks with conviction and an accent that suggests her heritage (linguistic and otherwise) is unrelated to that of the other characters. (Their actual differences are more that of temperament.) S rises to a seated position, back to the audience, and begins to distribute small white linens that had been concealed beneath her chest in her huddled position. The linens are carefully rolled and placed side by side to form the lineaments of a snug, rectangular enclosure. (Like a home or a fort.) When the last linen is laid out, she is directly facing the audi-ence and the music ends. It is as though she stares out a window over a placid landscape which she addresses.

S.
(As though to mark the completion of her task) There. *(Now, as though to indicate the newly generated exterior space)* Here and there went the air.

Light falls on Q, who had been obscured in the darkness, standing, in the dark space over S.'s shoulder. Also simply attired but in a darker hue than S's dress, Q speaks forward, to no one in particular.

Q.
Bombast!

S. *(Calmly describing some commotion in the distance)*
Dogs nip at it now.

Q. *(Also notices the commotion, narrating, slightly animated)*
Fast! Quicker! Quickly...

S.
It's insipid.

Q.
With feeling! Aplomb! Which is which? What do I know? What
difference would it make? What's insipid is the presumption of
distance when we are each and all perfectly familiar. From the per-
spective of life, don't forget, there is a very short list of elements,
and each of them is well known, each in the very same way. Am I
speaking to you? Do I exist?

S.
The air you breathe is a sinister smoke that shines, forgetfulness
briefly after.

Q.
Once I *was* certain. Those were the days, surely. The last place on
earth; simple continuity. But that kind of certitude is your mode,
not mine. Shouldn't we have things in common?

S.
It's said darkness hovers out there in the poetry of dramatic
interiors. Civility is a notion triggered by hypnogogic phenomena.
Every civilian is a hypnogogic trace of a better time. Every subject

a middle class. The dollar is psychosomatic. Looking to find or looking to see—no matter—we are confined to breathe. *(Appearing to recognize something else in the distance)* There.

Q. *(Goads)*
Is that blood in your throat as you try to speak? Is that blood in the snow? Is that snow? Some synthetic particulate, perhaps?

S.
Blighted tomatoes. Blooms of some sort. Nebulous—

Q.
Your proclamations are too ministerial, superannuated.

S. *(No longer speaking past him)*
In *this* language there are *only* images. *Were* I to make proclamations, rather than to think, the effort would swallow itself. I remain prone to the spasms to which deduction leads. My immunity *(inhaling to catch her breath)* is to causes, not effects. To you and your world I lie, like hotel linens to housekeeping. It's a question of tact.

Q.
Just feeling futile I get to feeling hoarse. In the beginning was auto-immunity. Alive and pleased to be living, S is *for* us. S is the salacious industry of belonging to bone. S for us is meat. Flesh for us is neat. S is furnished, a furnishing, upholstered with nourishing attributes.

S.
The third person speaks in red ink. You're so needy. You're no different from a family cat, in that. Even when you want to *be* alone it's that you *need* to be *left* alone.

Q. *(Knowing she's right, so trying to bait her by way of distraction)*
Our insouciance, their abundance, haters and claptraps, the generation gap.

S. *(She bites. Facing him)*
The titular!

Q.
The technonymous!

S.
Is that homely nub the tongue or the slogan?

Q.
Ah, parallelism! Again!

S.
Are you trying as you please rather than what pleases?

Q.
Continue!

S.
The investigator seeks motive. The prosecutor proves intent.
Nothing continues but reflection.

Q.
A rousing romp, a meandering vamp, a roiling rave, a seemly tryst in a mealy mist. A list of identical emissions!

S.
    Ditto plates
    Erudite

Lit abashed pink
With inference

Q. *(Exiting)*
Called back…[i]

S.
It's said darkness hovers out there in the poetry of dramatic interiors, a civilizing of the essay. If soliloquies are essays, poetry is not overheard *in order to be* audible. Some poets see what they do in every kind of poetry, so that they can both acknowledge and correctly identify various poetries, yet they insist on speaking of, about, and on behalf of poetry per se. The foundation of this egotism is so deep, it is a kind of anthropomorphism. The academic study of poetry is now mainly under the purview of creative writing rather than language and literature departments (the "language" moniker increasingly dropped in the 70s and 80s as creative writing and modern languages each consolidated institutional resources). Credentializing presumes competition, contestation, yet argument has been displaced by awards, prizes, secret committees. Experiment is hampered by competitive impulses (again the hard sciences show the way). College textbooks are now retailed by big box stores and one-stop sites that act according to the vicissitudes of supply and demand rather than curricular need. U.S. dollar hegemony [*Q enters*] coincides with the entrepreneurial spirit of versification, which is the new interiority (again the French show the way).

Q.
I have a poem on this subject.

As I was going down impassive rivers,
Determined by supply and demand based on market funda-

mentals,
Yelping redskins had taken them as targets,
Fundamentals that affect supply and demand.

I was indifferent to all crews,
As the dominant reserve currency,
When with my haulers this uproar stopped,
the US share of global exports (US$781.1 billion). Out of a
    world total

And into the furious lashing of the tides,
($1.257 trillion out of a world total of $6.65 trillion)
I ran! And loosened peninsulas
While 30 percent of the world's population lived on less
    than $1 a day.

The storm blessed my sea vigils.
Ever since 1971, when U.S. president Richard Nixon took
    the dollar off
Eternal rollers of victims,
At the end of World War II, the dollar has,

Sweeter than the flesh of hard apples is to children,
Produce. The dollar, now a fiat currency,
Washed me of spots of blue wine
and the status of the U.S. as the leading debtor nation. The
    U.S.,

And from then on I, bathed in the Poem,
GDP of $9 trillion,
Devouring the green azure where, like pale elated
things that dollars can buy, the world's

Suddenly dyeing the blueness, delirium
advantage; they compete in exports to capture needed dol-
    lars to service
Stronger than alcohol, vaster than our lyres,
sustain the exchange value of their domestic currencies.

I know the skies bursting with lightning, and the waterspouts
central banks must acquire, and hold dollar reserves in cor-
    responding,
And dawn as exalted as a flock of doves,
pressure to devalue a particular currency the more.

I have seen the low sun spotted with mystic horrors,
that in turn forces the world's central banks to acquire and
    hold more,
Resembling actors of very ancient dramas,
hegemony, which is created by the geopolitically construct-
    ed peculiarity!

I have dreamed of the green night with dazzled snows,
Everyone accepts dollars because dollars can buy oil. The
    recycling of—
The circulation of—unknown saps,
Of the oil-exporting cartel.

I followed during pregnant months the swell,
Capital accounts. Even after a year of sharp,
Dreaming that the luminous feet of
56 percent premium compared with emerging markets

struck against, you know, unbelievable Floridas
growing at a pace on par with the growth of the quantity of
    dollars…U.S.

Skin! Rainbows stretched like bridal reins
despite recent retrenchment in which entire sectors suffered
    some!

I have seen enormous swamps ferment, fish-traps
from 1990 through 2001,
Avalanches of water in the midst of a calm
country index posted a return of only 12.4 percent even
    without counting!

Glaciers, suns of silver, nacreous waves, skies of embers!
The U.S. capital-account surplus in turn finances the U.S.
    trade
Where giant serpents devoured by bedbugs
When oil is denominated in dollars!

I should have liked to show children those sunfish
And the more the U.S. prints
Foam,
dollar policy gives the U.S. a double win.

At times a martyr weary of poles and zones,
state action, as opposed to the mere surrender of state sov-
    ereignty to market forces,
Brought up to me her dark flowers with yellow suckers
by one single government

Resembling an island tossing on my sides the quarrels
Framed 11 years later, the U.S. founding fathers
And I sailed on, when through my fragile ropes
abhorrence of trade monopoly and government policy in
    restricting

Now I, a boat lost in the foliage of caves,
Which was practiced by all the major powers of the time, it
    is necessary,
I whose water-drunk carcass would not have been rescued

related to mercantilist issues of trade restraint;
Free, smoking, topped with violet fog,
By big business monopolies or by other governments
Bearing delicious jam for good poets,

remained higher in value than its imports, the surplus in
    that era being
Who ran, spotted with small electric moons,
Trade surplus in gold.
When Julys beat down with blows of cudgels,

More gold. The importing regions
Trembled, hearing at fifty leagues off
Free-fall devaluation (not unlike that faced today by many).
I, eternal spinner of the blue immobility,

building factories to produce for export, so despite plentiful
    iron ore,
Have seen sidereal archipelagos! and islands'
finished iron goods:
—Is it in these bottomless nights that you sleep and exile
    yourself,

disadvantaged trade relationship?
But, in truth, I have wept too much! Dawns are heartbreak-
    ing,
decreed the Iron Act, forbidding the manufacture of iron
    goods.

Acrid love has swollen me with intoxicating torpor.

Smith favored an opposite government policy!
If I want a water of Europe, it is the black
policy that came to be known as "laissez faire" (because the
    English,
A squatting child full of sadness, releases

English name). Laissez faire, notwithstanding its literal
    meaning of
No longer can I, bathed in your languor, O waves,
counteract mercantilism, Neo-liberal free-market economists,
Cross through the pride of flags and flames,

they propagandize "laissez faire" as no government interfer-
    ence in trade.[ii]

S.
And I have one on exteriority and interiority.

the hand that slants
the sea
slants tandems
to hand
planned here adjacent
to light

in planned tandems
light to
light in planes
it planned
the hand adjacent
that hand

the light hand
slants it

Let me paraphrase: Because you can't choose misery, you must always believe you are in the right. Contesting what, exactly? But you cannot know what. And you cannot know if this is so, or if you are right, or miserable for that matter, by learning of a wrong (whether a wrong you commit or a contradicted belief). This is why essays want to be the antidote to didactic poetry; their claims are not epistemologically operative, their opinions, their warrants, their flourish. Instead, the essay is its logic, its frolic, its experience which, seen in profile, appears as argumentation or gauze (to stop the brain drain luddites prophesize).

I will speak of, about, and on behalf of the essay. This is not only tolerable but actually warranted by being no essayist, and hav-ing been primarily identified as a poet, though I am really just a metaphysician.

Essays are the least constructed of the genres but most contingent upon the others. Their formlessness entails risk, which is what it means to essay something, of course. Homage and violence (even when neither is felt) reciprocate as essays. All prefatory matter is retrofit to essays (the next scene answers to this soliloquy). Essays are purely expressive. They are always self assigning (blame).

The experience of certainty is so rare that it induces déjà vu; its sole expression is morality. Morality's chief mode is prohibition, not essay. Not every president is a celebrity. Not all infamy is known. What stands for a temperament is everything frivolous in essays. Essays never write "for example" or "in my opinion." Though an essay can wish to be succeeded (by other acts and oth-er essays, by precedence, by presidents and speech writers), the

17

disinherited essay is the most pliable and most plausible. Though it insists there has been no misunderstanding, it finds it *must* insist on this nonetheless. In the absence of family resemblance, its truth claims are as steadfast as they are vacuous. Ambivalence is impossible without revision. The successful essay is recreational; fantasy is its mode. Infinite loops. Recognition as new life.

The elementally heraldic *poise* of baby boomer essays became the post-modern essay of exception and redistribution, porous and congested along a continuum of millennial neutrality. Both are basically pop. Evidently Marc Bolan claimed the valor of continuity when calling Rod Stewart "the Ethel Merman of rock," in the continuous distance between "Nijinsky Hind" and "Bang a Gong." Frolic is essayistic effort.

What is the relationship between medium and genre? Witness what it takes new media to forge: Etsy, Kickstarter, Lulu, Zazzle and Paypal. The commodification at last of the means of production lends a certain affluence (a platform) to essays. Once you've seen what you're looking at, the effort is immaterial. What is the difference between effort and essay? The latter is the possibility to fail in the sense of the former.

Since all the arts have tended to exploit their own media to the point of independence, the fact can be better used to prove that none of the arts is literally imitative than to furnish a reason for drawing hard and fast lines between them.[iii]

If there is nothing but experience (lived or cathected), and essays are definitively hypothetical, hence experimental, can there be inauthentic experiences? Can darkness hover? Can smoke shine? Can tomatoes bleed if their skins are red?

Act One: Scene Two

S enters several times, each identical in every way and finally assumes "child's pose," but facing us. Lights out. She rises to reveal a laptop computer which opens as she rises, a glow against her dress. The machine emits the identical passage of string music as opened scene one. It's best if this can be recorded for use in each iteration of S's entrance here; the action and diegetic music comprise a loop. The theater space is dark except for the black or blue (blank) LED screen of the laptop and otherwise silent for the duration of the passage on the violin. Black out. Dimmest lights rise to reveal S holding Q's petrified face in her hands. In his mouth is stuffed one of the linens. S breathes comfortably but audibly, signaling her immunity to the air. Black out.

This happens only once: S enters a small child. Nothing stokes a grave temper like the recognition of being illustrative. The diegetic loop above condensed in recognition of its looped character becomes the non-diegetic whorl that conventionally signals a flashback in a film. S recognizes that she, now "being in her very young living," is the product of a flashback, and so she has gotten ahead of herself. (The immortality implied by her immunity to the air she breathes pitches her into temporal chaos, and most of the effort in her living is concerned with avoiding the anxious recognition of this chaos. Here we have the only pure example of this anxiety, though a mixed form is decisive in the final scene of the play.) In her lecture "Plays," Gertrude Stein cites a passage from The Making of Americans *to illustrate the "difference between completion and relief" as the "difference between emotion concerning a thing seen on the stage" and that of a "real presentation," relief and completion respectively. Abandoned by her peers in the rain on a muddy street, young Martha Hersland cries out in bitterness, "I have throwed the umbrella in the mud." This (unobserved) act announced (yet recognized) completes the emotion. S will fail to find relief in dragging her linen through the mud. In subdued disgust she says, "plausibility and fate confused make foul weather. I will put my furnishings out into the street."*

Q.

A devious officiant who knows no restraint pronounces one from birth. Yet men make poor familiars. The lesson then is don't quote the good doctor. Don't repeat your lessons. (Lie to the medical establishment.) Quote the literature back to your physicians, attorneys, instructors… (everyone dies miserably.) Express your refusal with inscrutable pallor designed to imperil your interlocutor, who'll accuse you of androgyny and delusion. Don't listen. In lockdown no one listens, to remain men among them. In the cultural capitol of the most indulgent and entitled nation, no diaper changing stations in the museum restrooms for men. Not the Whitney nor the New Museum. Etc. Men and boys get down on the floor to be biometrically verified. Under regimes of global capital, men are boys ahead of time. (Anyone objecting to the use of the plural—that global capital demands a single regime— forgets that superficial nuances are introduced to prioritize the squalid comforts of "culture," distracting attention from and by the servitude of cultural production.) Whatever appears to be an enthusiasm is previously stifled. Everything about boys becomes paradigmatic. Porn becomes exemplary.

Paradigmatic boy enters. He has an essay he's written, entitled "Porn Is Great," from which he reads:

> Porn is great. All porn is great. All porn is equally great. All porn is equally great if it does what it's doing, turning you on. This is why porn is a function and not a product. Bodies in porn merely function. Acting is the furthest thing from their minds; bodies are mindless for this reason, in porn. But

when necessary they act and the acting is *great*, or when you can find it you think to yourself, this is great and very unlike lies or virtuosic thespian mannerism, because it forwards the plot, and there is no plot, so the acting is instrumental and collapses into the action. Bodies in porn insofar as they are pornographic are *pure* functions. If porn is not turning you on you do not blame porn but move directly to porn, which is turning you on. The great equivalence of bodies in porn resides in its singular function. This is why porn itself is a great equivalence; all bodies end up in porn and everyone is virtually pornographic, with unforeseen bodies in commotion with a gaze that replaces the psychosomatic erotic encounter between pantomime and shameful denouement. Porn lets guilt liberate and brings us together as consumers and citizen-subjects, in our most vivid aspect. This is why pornographic bodies are pseudonymous. It is how each finds its voice, as I had done, once porn made my own powers of discrimination not just dim but redundant.

Paradigmatic boy is interrupted here by vague sounds of a scuffle just out of sight.

Vignette:

Agnes Varda. *(Writes)*
Bird man, I love your tail.
It shines in the rising sun,
Gentle as a feather
And proud as a peacock.

R.
You can't be serious.

Varda.
A tail's not serious. It's superb or gay, but it's not serious.

R.
You don't understand men at all. *(Embraces Varda)*

Varda.
The feeling's mutual![iv]

Q. *(Improvising)*

I'm in an immodest orchard with a modest demeanor to match the grouchy patriarch who, while insisting on a vast property honed to the point of audacity, sired a few too many to leave time for attention to the grounds. So I do it instead. I am the gardener. He is a gentleman farmer.

Vignette:

Erika Mann.
No cock will crow for that,
No cock will crow for that,
The chickens don't say boo,
The cat could not care less,
For we all know it's true:
Each cleans up his own mess.[v]

Q. *(Soliloquizes)*

What if all possible conditions
pertaining in certain proportions,
prude ignorance, a happy outcome
and swift upshot equitably served

that tiny profession?

Bob Dylan knew Johnny B. Goode
was a folk artist too once
and pop twice ahead of time.
Prophecy and inspiration
are boys ahead of time,

whatever else it means to "go electric."
Lou Adler knew at least seven
types of ambiguity by the time
of *The Fabulous Stains*.
Municipal boys, district boys,

boy citizens benefit from
comparison... [Paradigmatic
boy is now listing, in the double sense
of making lists and obsessive shuffling,
and this list (twice over) comprises

a combined diagnosis and indictment
from which he'd take some arcane
refreshment in saturated colors (auto-
motive finish) or pink noise (traffic).]

Vignette:

Ito Hiromi.
Iiyoo

R.
Do-over

Ito Hiromi.
Iiyoo

iiyoo

R.
Do-over

Ito Hiromi.
Iiyoo
iiyoo

R.
Do-over

Ito Hiromi.
Iiyoo
iiyoo
iiyoo

R.
Do-over

Ito Hiromi.
Iiyoo
iiyoo
iiyoo
iiyoo

R.
Do-over

Ito Hiromi.
Iiyoo
iiyoo
iiyoo
iiyoo
iiyoo

R.
Do-over

Q.

A Form
To unchain Art from chattering
Initiation from Godgooderies
Power from stupidity
Wealth from ugliness[vi]

Act Two: Scene One

Productions in Chicago:

Audience and players without stepping out of character gather in Millennium Park, surround Anish Kapoor's *Cloud Gate*, each with a flash bulb in hand angled from a unique stance like gawking tourists enjoying fresh, lake air and a funhouse mirror. All bulbs are set off simultaneously. An aerial photograph is taken of the event and shows a poltergeist effect. S takes the photo home, acquires a self-portrait.

Productions in Madrid:

Audience members climb a ladder cautiously placed before *Guernica* and trace the hen. The first with egg on their face becomes S. Because museums in Europe frequently do not charge admission, the queue to trace *Guernica* will seem miniscule in comparison to the crowds gathered to see art rather than poets theater. But this only improves the odds of entering the script as S, who then exits into the painting to make way for herself.

Productions in Los Angeles:

S solicits treatments. The audience concurs. The winning treatment comprises the experience of winning. It's a bargain, the audience concurs.

Productions in Paris:

S is dressed in a stereotypical mime's costume complete with whiteface. She acts as a docent at the Square de la Petite Roquette, gesticulating a silent narrative of the early prison stay of

Jean Genet at the panopticon prison for children that stood here for decades—she and the audience stand amidst the playgrounds of the current park, small children all around, climbing over the swings and gyms. Standing before the plaque at the gate to the park, where the tour begins, S performs the box—poorly, too gracefully—to illustrate and pay tribute to the plight of the female resistance fighters who were imprisoned there during the German occupation. She leads the audience through the fountain just beyond the gates as the tour winds down, soaking everyone and disappearing into the water like a witch.

Productions in Prague:

Audience members are given solar filter lenses transmitting less than 0.003% (density~4.5) of visible light (380 to 780 nm) and no more than 0.5% (density~2.3) near-infrared radiation (780 to 1400 nm) before being led to stand before František Bílek's *Moses Dreaming of Adam.* Unbeknownst, the glasses had been dipped in a lethe-like serum which immediately returns each member of the audience to a dream state exactly replicating their very last dream, at which point their nomenclature awaits experience, though an exact fit is imminent and partially recognizable as they dimly emerge from this state to contemplate the even dimmer outline of the figure of Moses perceptible through the glasses. This premonition—a bad word for it, but a better one is sure to come—registers as a trivial menace or a kind of cramp. S is everything everyone is about to say.

Productions in London:

The theater and its scenario—that is, the house and its inhabitants—enter the transverse realm of cinema, Derek Jarman's *Jubilee*: specifically the super-8 scene of a bonfire featuring Amyl Nitrate, the historian, dancing a ballet beside "the boys." This scene elaborates on and foreshadows the scope of the tenacious grip of lucre on the imagination of temporality—not only history, but time itself, signaled by the classical masque dangling above the flaccid penis of one of the brother-lovers, as well as the sheen of decay over both the visuals and the soundtrack (deeply romanticized ennui—lugubrious nostalgia). We hear Amyl utter the line "Carnation from Floris: not all the good things have disappeared" in the voice of S and recognize we are the kidnapped young women, "punk" hooligans, attending a lesson in the hovel Amyl shares with Bod (Elizabeth I's doppelganger), Mad, Chaos, Crabs, and the boys. We hear this line again in voice-over as the car is pulling up to Borgia Ginz's estate in the gated community of Dorset, after the girls have sold out to the media machine. Amyl's obsession with the destruction of civilization through commercialism, on one hand, or through ennui on the other sits uneasily beside her adoration of all things flash. She is distraught when her Winston Churchill mug breaks. She loves expensive French perfume and enjoys the help of a French au pair. Yet she is not at all bothered by this fundamental contradiction. Mad's take on history is quite different, it seems. Mad duplicates the contradiction. "This is how to compress [history]," she says, "you forget it." But she doesn't advocate the abolition of memory so much as the destruction of half-remembered artifacts. She sets light to Amyl's *Teach Yourself History* book. Viv, the "artist" is a romantic. She's not nostalgic, but she believes and invests in love. She and the boys have a tender affair. She says to them, "I know [Mad] is right, that's what upsets me." Theater's allusive texture is transformed into didacticism in cinema. S is Amyl, but also Viv, Mad, and the boys themselves (not a resolution of their conflicting traits, but a combination). And we know this as we come out of the screen back into the theater. S does not acknowledge this collective epiphany, but why should she? She resolves the known, not the spasm of the onset of knowledge. She is beyond irony.

Productions in Tokyo:

In Tokyo, this play can only be produced as Sunday matinees in Yoyogi Park.

Productions in Edinburgh:

Audience members are each assigned a linen edifice identical to those used to construct S's enclosure; they strip and don them. All are walked to Castle Rock where they construct an exact facsimile of Edinburgh Castle composed of the repurposed basalt plug. In the end, the model and the sculptural artifact are completely level with each other, and with the city. S is entrusted as sentinel in lieu of any historic landmark.

Productions in Jamaica:

The ruins of Edinburgh Castle in St. Ann's Parish mark the home of the so-called "Mad Doctor" or "Mad Master" Lewis Hutchinson, the island's first serial killer, whose botched escape by boat pitted Scotsman against Scotsman in a legal proceeding wherein the testimony of Hutchinson's unwilling accomplices—his stock of African slaves—was perfunctorily dismissed as hearsay. When governments divide, arm, and deprive their citizens, Hutchinson's entrepreneurial spirit seeps about. S, as Amyl Nitrate, speaks these lines from atop the ruins of Hutchinson's fortress. "See 'London,' i.e. didacticism."

Productions in Sao Paulo:

S is time. As a means of character development, audience members converge on Jorge Macchi and Edgardo Rudnitzky's *Last Minute*. This installation translates texture into sound via a

sensor on the end of a giant second hand, ticking away each min-
ute, each minute itself sonically replenished—starting from silence.
Audience members assume child's pose, each with one of S's
linens in hand, in a circle surrounding the sweep of the piece. By
scouring with the linens the stone surface of the floor beneath the
sensor, the audience inscribes an utterance befitting their most
benevolent impression of S, that is, a phrase in her own voice that
she utters freshly 60 times each hour, perpetually, a phrase whose
every possible implication matches her traits to our anticipation.

Productions in New York:

S is hawking souvenirs at Ellis Island. They are genitally
precise statuettes depicting the bronze Smithtown Bull, found in
the same Long Island town where John Ashbery and James Schuy-
ler set their collaborative novel, *A Nest of Ninnies.* Each year, cock
and balls are painted traditional holiday colors: red and green
around Christmas, orange and black on Halloween, and so forth.
Not only does the reduced scale concentrate the optical magne-
tism of the bull, but the statuettes are sold with something like an
Easter Egg color-by-numbers kit, much pink, much blue. The bull's
name is Whisper and, according to legend, an English settler by
name of Smith was offered any and all lands then belonging to the
first nations of the island that he could traverse astride his Whis-
per.

Productions in Örebro:

In 2011 the *Big Yellow Rabbit,* by Florentijn Hofman, was
placed in the square just behind the 1865 statue of Engelbrekt
Engelbrektsson, the great leader of an eventually quashed peas-
ant/miner's rebellion. Engelbrekt's hatchet is precariously poised
at the giant plush toy's perineum. The rich yellow shingles forming

the surface of the rabbit were made by local, volunteer laborers. Here, the scale of the piece reorients the attention of passerby, transforming the focal point(s) of the site, shrinking the sky above and the air all around. The toy has seemingly dropped from the hand of a gargantuan toddler, and the texture of the shingles implies a chemical reaction with the atmosphere during its freefall, as though it had passed through a sick sky, dimming and dampening the presumably glowing lemon custard sheen of the animal's native pelt. S reaches for and removes the hatchet, making away with it and returning to the stage.

Productions in Moscow:

S hawks souvenirs outside the Kremlin. Tiny hatchets.

Productions in Bologna:

In the Sanctuary of Santa Maria della Vita stands Nicollo dell'Arca's *Lamentation Over a Dead Christ*, six terracotta figures surrounding the corpse of the messiah. St. John the Evangelist stands at the center, his chin in the palm of his right hand, head turned slightly toward the scene, his eyes further turned to view it. When passing a skyscraper at close range, pedestrians looking upward at the edifice will sometimes perceive the whole structure to be teetering over (from the top of a tall cliff, one sometimes perceives themselves as toppling over). From Christ's perspective, St. John's arm might seem to lift straight up, detaching his head from his body, presenting, like a lamp, himself to view. His left hand holds his robe before his midriff. The beige hue of his robe (like much of the rest of the piece) bears a visual, choreographic resemblance to S in Act One: Scene One. But no Bolognese production need emphasize this self-evident resemblance.

Productions in Sarajevo:

The library that was destroyed in the Siege should be ritually repopulated by the cardinal initials that provide the title of the play. Improvised permutations and imagined variations, in the tradition of Jackson Mac Low's list of kinds of light (see *The Light Poems*), should be freely and locally devised. UNESCO should fully and copiously fund any and every such production.

Some localities:

Some works exude their own elaborations, but it should be usefully and not exploitatively suggestive to mention such sites in particular. After all, they serve as hosts for external dramatic sequences. Here is how a short list of such locations and landmarks begins: The Black Hole of Calcutta; Ernst Thalman Statue and Park in Berlin; The Black Brigade Monument project in Smale Riverfront Park, Cincinnati, OH…

Tyrone Williams was commissioned to write epigraphs for the Black Brigade Monument, and revisions to those he submitted were requested for the sake of accessibility. Here is an unrevised version as gauge of the tandem between the monumental and the sanctioned:

Child,
     your father
   my husband
     sleeps far
  from us
     this first of
  heaven knows
     how many
nights.

Bangkok:

"DON'T TOUCH MOTHER OF PEARL," reads the large red placard at the feet of the Reclining Buddha of the Wat Pho. The mother of pearl inlay depicting the auspices of the Buddha, together with 108 bronze bowls (where unofficial offerings are collected from tourists and other pilgrims). Productions in Bangkok should consist in exponential reductions of such points into the cardinal initials that provide the title of the play. The specific formulae, or particular exponents, may be improvised according to the familial drama's implied histrionics. Take the spirit for the letter.

Seoul:

It should be possible to enjoy a commanding view of the DMZ from the Park Hyatt's 24th floor lobby.

Copenhagen/Kimballton, IA:

It should be possible to enjoy a commanding view of the Langelline waters from the vantage point of Edvard Eriksen's *Little Mermaid.* But numerous renditions, beheadings, dismemberments, and coats of paint have compromised the historical continuity of this perspective, or rather problematized its plausibility. The Situationists cut off her head, and a group of radical feminists once cut off her arms. After one such incident, the children of the city appeared weeping on televisions throughout the country and the culprit felt so guilty that head and limbs were returned anonymously. If a copy exists in, say, a rural Iowa town, or the Danish pavilion of Shanghai's Expo 2010, among others, then all the same should be possible; the plausibility of the statue's fabulous compossibility. Asger Jorn and Guy Debord's *Fin de Copenhague* mechanized action painting, printing or ascribing it from atop a ladder with pails of lithographic inks. The book's radical luxor however comes across quaintly expressive despite its very dé-tournement. Pranks rely on a certain plausibility that should save them from flamboyance. Elegant simplicity is what works. They have nothing to express but a sober manqué. Finally, a series of pranks amounts to a wiki, a mimetic stage, more serious than history, as Aristotle decreed, because fiction is principled instead of veritable. As S maintains, while fellow metaphysicians draw an absolute distinction between extensive (physical) and intensive (psychic) states of being, she finds in the opposition an unexam-ined, axiomatic hierarchy that can fall to either state, and from which the other state of being is derived: a crude materialism or a mystic idealism. Circumstances constrain the imagination, and circumstances are anything plausible. But S has found fictive circumstances to liberate matter from states and instead relies on the dynamic passage from one to the next. The next is never the other. Hegel, idealist dialectician and bastard spirit of Situation-ists, granted to things the indetermination of intensive states, and like so much spilt ink, tricked S into herself, the none-other-than, split at the midriff between regimes of oxygenation.

from   Tan Lin

subject   Re: Cities, Public Art, Landmarks

to   You

sorry to take so long on this

CCTV in Shanghai

Tan

On SaturdayMay 19, 2012, at 4:09 PM, Patrick F. Durgin wrote:

> Friends,

> I am asking for suggestions concerning a project I am working on. I am drawing up a list of world
> cities and a piece of public art in each of these cities (or a work of art living in that city that somehow
> belongs to it, e.g. Guernica lives in Madrid and that is a present fact about it). I then draw from the
> list to create a brief dramatic sequence taking that site/work as the setting, usually involving the
> artwork in a way that is entirely outside its function as an art-work. In lieu of artworks, or even cities,
> I am interested in specific landmarks that might be ripe to host a dramatic sequence of some kind. I
> don't want to say more than this--let's keep this very loose--but please take a second to reply with a
> place name, etc., even if these are vague. The further from home, the better.

> Thanks,

> Patrick

Productions in Minneapolis:

Any production in the Twin Cities will involve a dras-
tic distillation of Claus Oldenberg and Coosje Van Bruggen's
Spoonbridge and Cherry, in the sculpture garden of the Walker
Art Center. First, melt down the spoon and recast as cups numer-
ous enough to serve each member of the audience, as well as the
players. Then juice the cherry. To cool, freeze the fountain and
distribute ice—crushed for convenience—among the cups. Serve
solemnly, as this is communion with language, with S, and with
the plastic arts—combined to form the beautiful as the poet mau-
dit, Charles Baudelaire declared, distilled from the manners of
everyday life to reveal the eternal verities of beauty. This produc-
tion moves from the cosmetic to the cosmos, rendering *PQRS* a
neo-modernist drama forged from the dregs of the contemporary.
PQRS is a rapid prototype, a dumb fogger, a rounding error, a
set of advices spoken past whatever it says it is. *PQRS* is a set
of characters; like weakly defined hues in a colorist kunstwerk,
initials spell themselves. They don't ooze relevance and there are
no booby traps.[vii] *PQRS* is lens flare. S is fair to misty. Intention is
sex, more pith and less aura.

Act Two: Scene Two
REMAKES

Q.

In Stanislaw Lem's novel *Solaris*, Rheya is an iteration of an "imperfect god," though not in an attempt to scale either God or nature toward the human. Even human stupidity relents, but the adaptability of Rheya is relentless. She and the sentient ocean of planet Solaris are extrasensory projections linked to the conscience of the cosmonauts peering down from the orbiting station, also called Solaris. The Solarists, as they are called, have forfeited life on Earth for the possibility of contact with the planet. Most likely to make that sacrifice would be persons fleeing a guilty conscience or maintaining a missionary zeal ill-suited to the inevitable diplomacy of earthly existence (these reasons are of course wholly compatible). (Lem devises a feature of planet Solaris that resembles solar flares, the "mimoid," that simply rehearses the loneliness of the demiurge; with no model nor audience, what good is it to be the Creator?)

Rheya's doppelganger Hari, in Andrei Tarkovsky's cinematic adaption of the novel, is "imprinted time." The intergalactic psychologist who happened to have quasi-intentionally led her to suicide some years back is, with his understandably perturbed conscience, the author of this iteration and/or imprint. Yet the filmmaker amplifies *her* experience, and forces us to recognize her fate without the satisfaction of witnessing it play through. She is a failure who can't be allowed to fail, because she is always this or that side of human. Kelvin, the psychologist, is, rather than wracked with guilt, either (in Lem) at loose ends with his ethos as a scientist (the burden of first person narration is one culprit) or (in Tarkovsky) engaged in an elaborate displacement of that guilt onto familial imaginations. A made thing is an evolution of a desire for repetition that itself adapts to desire the thing. In none of this has a creative faculty emerged, hence we take mimesis as a principle of adaption between media (which, if they don't already differ—say, I write a poetic adaption of an essay—would have to be made to differ). The source of desire is a social arrangement, so remakes are always better than their sources, always contemporary rather than original, and we make a fetish of media with respect to whatever originality (creativity) we still consider lost (like Rheya's humanity). Hari can't fail to live, can't be made to die or cease recurring, whereas humans fail simply by virtue of their mortality, though failure itself is nothing compared to the dread of living in (as) its wake.

So while Lem's mimoids remind us that Rheya can only be a reconstructed concept of a bad conscience, Tarkovsky's Kelvin, in attempting to hide from her this fact (upon her resurrection, stashing the redundant garments she'd left behind), knows that he nurses his conscience by loving her, not the other way around. This is what is evoked when, while Kelvin's Virgil attempts to distract him from his morbid pining with the sensible expedient of deferring such questions until he finds himself "at the end of life," Kelvin can know what Hari's failure defined. Not only do we not know when we are at the end of life, but that ignorance "makes us practically immortal." The slow (not langorous, but fixed) pan into Kelvin's ear cavity as he sits in profile—with the expression of a very satisfied thinker—sends us from a single extant shawl to the island in his mind that renders Earth an ersatz Solaris.

John Cage remade the lecture as mesostic renga using "as maximal source" Thoreau's lecture-cum-*Essay on the Duty of Civil Disobedience*. The intention was to "make the earth safe for poverty without dependence on government," *Anarchy*. What governs the individual in *Civil Disobedience*? A remake: "The progress from an absolute to a limited monarchy, from a limited monarchy to a democracy, is a progress toward a true respect for the individual. Is a democracy, such as we know it, the last improvement possible in government? Is it not possible to take a step further towards recognizing and organizing the rights of man?" (Thoreau's repetitive walks are not "progress" nor scientific reduplication.) In Cage's "way of writing which though coming from ideas is not about them," intention is what is happening for us (poverty); motivation is estimates of the future and projections from the past (safety). Reconstituting a source, itself a made thing, leads to the ambivalence of participatory "open texts" as musical score—the most non-intentional compositional procedures are the most responsible to their motivations. The mimetic ensemble remakes the earth. "that government is Best which governs least and i"

"i," the dangling integer/subject (neither and both an equation or list) describes some certainties. Markets are malign. Competition does not reveal merit. (What about disagreement, debate, critique? But the impresario of contest is a scoundrel for making any foe into a cowering incompetent; but contests are based on agreement as to what victory requires, and the competition reinforces these uncontested critical values, rather than taking exception to them. Individuals can share values; singularities cannot. Individualism and markets, like innovation, are contrary to the logic of remakes.) What if we are naturally competitive? But who still believes in social Darwinism? I would have thought everyone knew it to be an excuse to broadcast a notion of human nature, just to institutionalize it as creativity or intelligence, of which there is neither evidence nor use, of which there is therefore no experience. These things are nonexistent. What is a made thing? There is nothing but experience. There are only authors.

A musical interval is an applied misrecognition. It is barely there. It is like the physical memory of a musician: the same without becoming mimetic. The physical memory of a musician is this same anticipatory awareness of a critic. Predispositions determine one's attention to the world. Physical memory and predatory intent imitate one another in the presence of these moments of noticing what the mind-body specifies. If we equate imitation with predilection and encounter instead of with mimesis, Gertrude Stein's early portrait—of she and her brother Leo and their decisive falling out over the primary tenets of literary cubism—"Two" says the opposite. It is possibly the most exhaustive syllabic implosion in prose of any language. Almost 200 dense pages of sentences like, "She was one and sound sounding was coming and coming out of her sound was sounding and she was one and being that one and sound sounding she was needing being that one and needing being that one she was needing and she was needing needing to be one having sound coming out of her, needing sound sounding needing to be one, she was needing to be one, she was needing, to be one, she was needing sound coming, she was needing, she was one, she was needing sound coming, she was needing, she was one, she was needing sound sounding, she was needing sound sounding, she was needing sound sounding, she was needing sound sounding, she was needing sound sounding to be one, she being one she was needing to have sound sounding, she was needing sound to be coming out of her, sound." "Two" is a single thrust of mimetic permutations laying flat all available contingencies. It traces the impasses and buries the gullies between ripples of dissent, as familiarity discovers itself to have lost its bearings completely. But it *says* this. The text succeeds its own conditions. That is why it is like sheet music.

After "Two," for her or anyone else, it becomes possible to imitate (former) selves. This is evident in late or at least later period masterpieces. I think of a couple of my favorite rock bands who, after a period of diminished returns, find something especially profound and outright indicative, but that we have never heard before. Sonic Youth's 2002 album closer "Sympathy for the Strawberry" is one. The album is *Murray Street*. The entirety of *The Real New Fall L.P. (Formerly Country on the Click)* is another. Both are examples of what children call a "do-over"; both have a former self. The recording of *Murray Street* was interrupted by the events of September 11th; their studio and hence the tapes etc. were just a few blocks from the WTC. It was all inaccessible for a time, and then work on the album resumed. A rough mix of The Fall album was leaked and widely circulated online, under the title *Country on the Click*. Then it was remixed and possibly to a significant extent rerecorded. I can make these observations but I am not sure yet what they mean, this having been prior to their being what I make of them here.

Something about our own authority makes us queasy. Liberation theology is the most salient solution yet devised, a sort of mimoid culture. In Culture's "Two Sevens Clash," the millennial prophecy of its "version," "Prophecy Reveal," concludes its litany of scripture, "Take it or leave it!" That year, Richard Hell sang of his "Blank Generation," "I can take it or leave it each time." Having it both ways, or ever ("each time") the same, is repugnant. Johnny Ramone can claim mere "integrity" has held his group intact in light of Blondie's success with black music, the disco hit "Heart of Glass." Yet in 1979, The Ramones will cover "Baby, I Love You," with Phil Spector at the controls. And Ronnie Spector will reemerge in the '80s to duet with Eddie Money, an ex-cop and classic rock staple from Buffalo. Culture is the motion sickness that serves as a prelude to the certainties we cannot authorize, the sickness that is only its symptoms but, like a mimoid, never reduplicated in experience.

Act Two: Scene Three

P and R are tied at the ankles and laboriously walking, often glancing upward into the distance as though through a blustery sky. Their gait is practiced. For a long time, they say only "left" or "right" to mark each step, until R breaks the monotony.

R.
Why couldn't I be John, James, Jimmy even?

P.
Q is for question, P is preternatural, R, my dear brother, is my coadjutor. You would sacrifice the moral authority of the letter for the spirit of a boy, a name for boyishness?

R.
Here we are, trudging through the so-called air, two to whom breathing is toxic and stillness is fatal. It's a bore. In lieu of a destiny, I've got to harbor wishes. If you won't even hear them, yet you keep calling this a collaboration…

P.
You know I'm the only one who breathes to die. You may not be immune, but suffering is life. You just chew on it. When you spit, boy ectoplasm comes out.

R.
As always, you underestimate how ambiguous the atmospheric conditions are.

P.
There's a paraphrase afoot! Step!…left, left, left… The strictest form attainable in an area where one can*not* work precisely![viii]

R.

The atmospheric conditions are ambiguous for the same reason
and to the degree that our relationship to one another's act of
trudging is ambiguous: How can one know more than their own
effort, to realize a simultaneous effort also propels them?

P.

Attraction and repulsion. Fort-da-fort-da. It's all psychodramatic
cliché. P is for psyche, R is for repetition. With us, even a rote jaunt
to the toilet reinforces a theory, seems to be the case, quivers with
immensity. S is for summary.

R.
So it is. S is for so. I is for is.

P.
Your existentialism isn't helping either.

R.
It's not mine, it's ours.

P.
You identify too avidly, dear brother.

R.

I am an alchemist. I make things identities. All identities are
forged; resenting the reminder that they are forged of semiotic
materials, we reincarnate. So welcome back, novice!

P.

A relationship between letters as redundant or impervious as S's
second entrance.

R.
As S's managing to be here.

P.
As S's managing to arrive.

R.
When S looks for you, brother, she finds only carnage. When we cultivate the earth, we're gnawed on, surrounded, and...

P.
We think we're herding and we're being corralled, maybe both at once. Heaven above and earth below.

R.
Redundancy is the curse of euphemism—it summarizes as it softens, sweetens as it stales. But I have tried to be an example to you, to matter. To force myself upon only that which is beneath us takes no agility, just the wish, and the soil of course must be thawed and bled—

P. *(Aside)*
...preposterous brother, bother, both...

R.
—until the next of kin takes your side of things.

Intermission: Metaphysics

A vocabulary that needs modulating needs an avid audience. At least once.

Only rivals converse. Soliloquy is rivalry surveilled.

Drama is a vocabulary modulated by rivalry (character entails antagonism). Character epitomizes its language. Dramatic norms limn impersonal eccentricities, swift swerves and singularities.

The ideal drama lacks all psychology. Its conflict is (purely) immanent to its action—supposition succeeds supposition without reflection in the least. The ideal drama is something never done well but then well enough done.

Every conviction is a matter of fact, but not every fact is convincing. What more is needed if not less perspective, minus audio? (Soliloquy is a plea for oversight.)

Rhythm is tempi disclosed by time's pitch, from grinding lenses, tapping toes, severed speaker cones, alternating current, elegiac routines.

Soliloquy is only the most lauded form of self involvement. What impresses most are our powers of surveillance, powerful enough to escape our own notice.

Familial disputes are affectless exertions monumentalized and restaged as emotion by the ritual theater and the lyric pitch alike. The amplifier converses. A voice projected into a house is a model of the only possible behavior: drama. What's overheard is insensible.

What's overheard is an image, not a lyric. Lyric as cosmetic reful-
gence. Discussion ruins an image. So its conditions are overwrit-
ten.

Theatrical productions are playwrights' reproductions. An audi-
ence is a fictive blank. The script is gratified by an empty page as
empty sets stage all tales.

All existence is audience to my recognition. Audience is task.
Intention is sex. Sex is essay.

Because you cannot choose misery, failure must be a matter of
obedience. In the same way, an audience is not so much finicky as
forgetful. Gertrude Stein said this.

Sweet William came to be about, dispersed, covered over the earth.
This is Sweet William's cameo.

S.W.
Why is a magic trick a trick? How are tricks? In what sense is a
marriage not a wedding? A recitation weds its words to a poem.
Any question of subject matter is always a trick question. *About*
also means dispersed, that to which no attention is owed, I sup-
pose. Depose the I to bring the dispersed to a point. What is the
role of artifice in concentrating matters otherwise diffuse? Do
they then matter? Or is it just me (that matters then)?[ix]

Act Three: Scene One

R. *(Hands wrapped in bloodied white linens)*
To be earth? Being anyone. Anyone at any moment a genuine
wondering, an honest day's work, what anyone would do—*(notices
he's alone and turns to face Q offstage—Q enters midsentence:)*
Hurry! Your little brother wants his humanity named—he's feeling
reflective and I'm dripping blood here!

Q.
You have no right to be so much his enemy.

R.
He has no enemy. R is for roundtable. Culpable—why, that's a
feminine rhyme!

Q. *(Redressing R's wounded hands)*
What about the right to an interior life? I think you're project-
ing. P is for projection, or project. You've made the youngest your
project, your human.

R.
I don't have projects. I work up to earth's demands.

Q.
By stifling atmosphere, choking shoots and culling blooms and…

R.
And what about you? You're miserable in the mornings, up all
night perfecting itunes playlists, curating dramas on tumblr,
admiring your cuticles. How do you decide it's time to turn in for
the night?

Q.

I have—I *will* have it all spelled out. That's what it means to suf-
focate: inhale all you will, exhalation's what fails. It's an embarrass-
ment of riches.

R.

A reiteration.

Q.

A global economy. Meritocracy presupposes oligarchy.

R.

Universal human rights. R is for right and there is an infinite
amount of me.

Q.

A delivery mechanism? *(Pause)* Hadn't thought of that, hmmm?

R.

No one thinks with their lungs. *Try* not to breathe. It can't be
done, except in childish protest. P is a child—effective protest re-
quires an audience, but P has no sense of that. Just an overbearing
interiority. The more you coddle him—

Q.

You're projecting!

R.

—the more constricted you become! *(Aside)* All I wanted was agit-
prop, hecklers…

Q.

Family dramas don't make poems. Orphans can't be poets. Poets
need letters and letters need spirits.

R.

S is for surrealism. Whether dodgy automatism or doctrinaire Marxist-Leninism.

Q.

Q is for quid pro quo, belles lettres, mid-American hospitality, pop mitigation, the linguistic turn.

R.

Bed and breakfast.

Q.

P is for professor. Hot air. It heats in the lungs and bloats. It burns.

R.

I have to take *your* word for it. Toxicity is *my* hypothesis.

Q.

But not a consequence—?

R.

For some. How do you think I get so much done out here? How do you think I heal? How do I regenerate?

Q.

If each day is a scene, this one is an exit. Each entrance a cure.

R.

I don't *wound*. I am my own understudy.

Q.

What do you need P for, then?

R.

P is for promise. I want to "show great promise." I want to build expectation. I want to answer an audience.

Q.

You can't make scare quotes with bandaged hands.

R.

Don't have to—my mind will do the talking. Instrumentality, despite the infirmity reminding me the somaform disintegrates and I'm left foolproof, infallible, exemplary!

Q.

Someone must fail. Failure has to exist. If it were you...I can say I failed but no one will permit me to believe this. You can't agree if I admit this. It's all temples and ruins, soliloquy or dialogue, anything incredible is permitted before the meritocracy will be suffered. This is why the meritocracy is the fundamental preserver of interiority and atmosphere.

R.

Is this what you're saying, you've failed?

Q.

Either way, it has to exist.

R.

On what terms? There are no global terms of failure. Only cycles. Emersonian circles. There is no provision for deciding, yes, this experience is genuine, that one is rarefied.

Q.

Reified.

R.
Quaint.

Q.
Does it matter to have spent your hours, days, and a life feeling
happy or sad?

R.
Not directly. These are private matters.

Q.
But I have neither the time nor the intelligence for indirection.
*Any*one needs unities, fate, plausibility.

R.
What does performance (art) have to do with linkage between
the rise of the romantic lyric and drama's autonomy (the advent
of "theatre")? Nothing much. Performance was a reaction to the
artwork's stasis where the ontological status of poems was never
a very well defined problem. Nonetheless, the voice that was once
an epiphenomenon of the hero as played becomes the displace-
ment of the dubious ontic status of a poem (before linguistics
could have come to rescue poetry). Because you cannot choose
misery, no one admits failure, even failure to exist. Poor, poor
poetry. So long, privacy! Hello pontifical interiors!

Q.
Poetry is the auto-immunity of private life. Fate is natural counting
(in the midst of life…etc.) I know a poem about knowing about
this:

> The face is not a collection of attributes
> It expresses itself
> It's going out

Of my mind
One look at it and my eyes roll back
To imitate my death

So bad tragedy
Is bad comedy
Is the poetry of dramatic interiors

You must know that one.

R.
It's not the same to hear you say it. Fate, then. I have tried to make it rhyme with quaint too long. S's influence. S is for supposition.

Q.
...S *(wistfully)*. S is the only storied one. S has fate.

R.
But S is fated also. S is for she.

Q.
S is the only storied one, two, three etc. But you have no experience of your own brother. Go ahead: call for your line! What you've memorized is the prompter's line, as it is cued and you complete the script of a memory, initials P, Q, and—

R.
My audience assures your presence, the present experience, and the properties of our language; our share in it.

Q.
S is for share.

R.
S is for scenery.

Q.

C is for council—conciliatory?

R.

Don't eulogize. Don't sweeten.

Q.

Another project of *yours*, I suppose. Forever young, regenerative. P is for puerile.

(R sits, seemingly fatigued.)

Prurient even.

R.

I am *so* fated. What I'm lacking is psychology.

Q.

Spell that!

R.

P is for psyche. Husbandry is my fate. But fate is no story. The minimal condition, maybe.

Q.

But something precludes story.

R.

Someone, anyone would, who could fail indeed…don't make me say it!

Q.

You're not special.

R.
I am species. I *have* to be *specific.*

Q.
That's brother's cause for acclaim, then? You face the chore of mortality for the sake of…*drama. (Joins R on the ground, inspects his hands and again replaces gauze/linens.)* For your own sake, say you spelled it and do something else.

R.
What would you be then—if I am what I am—

Q.
There must be brothers and mothers, failure, shadows—S is for shadow.

R.
Widow. Mistress. Mistrust. A shadow is the darkness hovering.

Q.
Your story can be…like you never notice shadows moving, only having moved against an invariable landscape is not beneath notice.

R.
But above knowledge—

Q.
I know. I speak these consoling words. I know…

R.
Having barely thought yet.

Q.
You yourself said, to be the earth is not to think, necessarily.

R.

To be relieved of a faculty that only mystified me.

Q.

Is that what this is? Relief? And how's *that* spelled?

Act Three: Scene Two
THE MAUDIT TRADITION

P.

But what is ennui, really? I'll tell you what it is: inequity of ethical license. Bratty·intolerance of roles assumed, human interest pages, contaminants, pundits, scribes, and pupils.

"Disease and mental instability cause health," declares "Mr. Linker" to his hoodlum pupils in Kathy Acker's *Blood and Guts in High School.* Acker aptly names her protagonist Janey's captor and pimp. Mr. Linker's brief cameo is a transition point, from Janey's abdication into the abject plight of womanhood to her "book report," a classic Acker moment of paratextual play with *The Scarlet Letter,* itself definitively linking the social enforcement of (misogynist) normalcy to the aesthetic enculturation of the citizen subject. A desperate humanist proselytizer, Mr. Linker's doctrine appreciates that, as "literature is the most abstract of the arts" because the "only art which is not sensual," and by virtue of his "materialist" training in "philosophy of psychology," "a body cannot live without disease." But when confessing his own infirmity, there seems to be a remarkable confusion between this white-slaver-lobotomist-summer-resort-operator (a Renaissance man) and his wife who died weaving him a rug or, "actually," she who "had been driven crazy" and institutionalized. The priceless virtue has ambiguous origins: "A healthy body in a healthy mind" becomes "A healthy mind in a healthy body"; or vice versa, each entwined priority means he has "returned to what he had been saying." Mr. Linker's tautology marks him a classic maudit, whose doctrine of self-pity lauds the things we profess to need and don't really want, poetry, for example. The highest, freest expression of human dignity: a nice place to elicit, but I wouldn't want to go there. Poetry stinks of the flowers of evil the better to imitate its own impossible ambivalence. Mr. Linker promulgates this ideology not as an act of resistance—no one in Acker's universe is capable of resistance as we'd like to fathom it—but as an object study in the darkest features of Darwinian benevolence. Mr. Linker is hardly a character. He is a caricature; due to Acker's singular and signature lack of moralizing character development, he remains a disembodied form. We are not invited to judge him as an extrapolation of lived experience. A technology of interpellation rather than a model of techne, he's not even Janey's antagonist, but an excessive inscriptional function, a functionary of the textual imagining of the paratextual section to come. The salutation marks him as fraudulent and ironizes our impulse to read him as an element of a *novel*, in the conventional sense of that term. Mr. Linker is a hermeneutic occasion for Janey's book report. Qua literary form, it is the supreme irony that Mr. Linker's squalid logic should not unfamiliarly sketch the relationship of textuality to embodiment.

When Arthur Rimbaud declared "je est un autre," he was not affirming a poetics of "introspection," his biographer Graham Robb was. This letting of signs to posterity is the flowering of the diabolical Romance the maudit celebrated. The continuity of the maudit tradition can be explained as history, not historically (to put the cart before the horse, as they did in the capital of the 19th century). Baudelaire let immanence—so what if it must be an "artificial paradise"?—sublimate his spectacular collusion. This is why Acker's linked retelling of the Rimbaud-Verlaine affair is signed *in memorium to identity*.

Judging from Baudelaire's prophetic statement, in *L'Art romantique*, about Modern Art's "essentially demonical" aspect, we can gather that the satanic is a buffer against ennui. Abject ennui (as opposed to bland double-entendres like "artist") precludes the absorption of proto-consumer culture's denigration of artistic material (while there was still specifically *artistic* material). Secret histories are claimed (say by Baudelaire, then Verlaine, Ginsberg, eventually Eileen Myles—see her piece on *Pull My Daisy* [which for good reason she entitled "Reunion"]) to both motivate and legitimize the creative process. The continuity of the maudit tradition might be the autopoetic conviction it harbors regarding its own existence (history). "Is holy holy?" asks Kerouac for Ginsberg in *Pull My Daisy*. It's a gag, as the maudit "Essence of Laughter" (Baudelaire) survives post-war American ennui. But the fascination with spontaneity is not reciprocated, being the gag is a footnote to "Footnote to Howl."

The footnote's effort is expository, while the essay's is, as mentioned elsewhere, a frolic. Yet essays do without psychology, and so they entirely lack portrayal and, to that extent, resist dramatization. Portrayals are characterological, but Mr. Linker, say, is more formal circumstance than active content. If he *had* character he'd portray the maudit. Without it, he enters fluidly and decisively that self-same tradition. To see him behind the characters L-i-n-k-e-r is to experience aspect blindness (the duckrabbit). Is he he? it? scapegoat? martyr? (In *The Birth of the Poet*, Cynthia asks, "Do I exist?") To dramatize him is to forego action. It calls for a "pure event," as defined by Gilles Deleuze in the 21st series of *The Logic of Sense*, as a "mobile and precise point" exemplified by the "psychopathology which the poet makes his own" (thinking here of Ginsberg and the superiority of Anglo-American literature in particular, made but not given), "where all events gather together in one [and] transmutation happens:"

> this is the point at which death turns against death; where dying is the negation of death, and the impersonality of dying no longer indicates only the moments when I disappear outside of myself, but rather the moment when death loses

itself in itself, and also the figure which the most singular life takes on in order to substitute itself for me.

The maudit tradition raises the question of resentment inevitably. It does not portray it but betrays that, in the lore of the cursed artist, a pathos *made* has consequences. It was against the reinforced inconsequentiality of poesis that the tradition found all the past virtually available, all the authority in the world.

Interlude

Q.

I have a poem on becoming an author, like my brother (R is for recitation), and my father before him *(Recites, to the tune of "12XU" by Wire)*:

> Since Marx's famous description of the talking commodity,
> I once heard a learned man say that time is nothing but the
>   movement
> we are accustomed to seeing, economic forms brought to
>   life. It is less common
> of the sun and the moon and the stars, but I
>
> however—to see such a form given life only to be put to
>   death—
> did not agree. Yet this is what we find in the name for a
>   contract.
> But we apprehend time only when we have marked motion
> on a real estate loan, a mortgage, which comes from the
>   French for "dead pledge,"
>
> marking it by before and after. And it is only when
> trying to understand why this particular contract should
>   take on such a mortal cast,
> we have perceived before and after in motion, that we say
>   that time has elapsed.
> The sixteenth-century jurist Sir Edward Coke explained, "It
>   seemeth that the cause why
>
> guilt is like the moral thread which duplicates the thread of
>   time,
> it is called *mortgage*, is for that it is doubtful whether the

Debtor will pay.
I once heard a learned man say that
at the day limited such summe or not, & if he doth not

time is nothing but the movement of the sun.
Pay, then, the Land…and the moon
is taken from him for ever, and the stars, but I did not agree.
And so dead to him upon condition, &c. And if he doth
    pay the money,

but we apprehend time only when we have marked motion,
then the pledge is dead as to the Tenant." The mortgaged
    property
marking it by before and after exists in an ontologically per-
    ilous realm,
and it is only when we have perceived before and after

alive to one but not another, rising from the grave and
    returning
in motion that we say that time has elapsed to life as it
    changes hands.
What is it about the real estate loan that makes all its paths
    lead to death?
Guilt is like the moral thread which duplicates the thread
    of time.

The connection between borrowing and burying is en-
    crypted
I once heard
in the etymology of the word
a learned man say "mortgage,"

but the language of horror that time is nothing
has also been manifestly present,

but the movement of the sun and the moon and the stars
in contemporary representations of the ongoing financial
    and credit crises. But I did not agree.

But we apprehend time only when we have marked motion
from the ubiquitous "zombie banks" to muckraker Matt
    Taibbi's description of Goldman Sachs as a "great,
    blood-sucking vampire squid," a discourse of the
    gothic, the uncanny,
marking it by before and after, and the terrifying is itself,
and it is only when we have perceived before and after in

the specter haunting late capitalism. In
motion that we say this essay, I argue
that time has elapsed,
that this discourse does not

merely reflect the anxiety and fear guilt is
associated with, current economic volatility, but
like the moral thread which duplicates the thread
is rooted in fundamental transformations in the economy

of time itself: specifically, the financialization of credit
    markets. And
I once heard a learned man say that the power of securi-
    tized debt to penetrate the very fabric of daily life,
that time, to understand the increasing inextricability
is nothing but the movement of the sun and the moon and
    the stars, but of horror and securitized credit, I turn to a
    text that

I did—brings them explicitly together: not
the 2009 horror film *Drag Me to Hell* (dir. Sam Raimi), in

which the standard tropes of the horror genre agree.
But we apprehend time only when we have marked motion,
    marking it by.
Before and after are repurposed

to represent the emerging horrors of our dangerous new
    economic order
and it is only when we have, in Raimi's film, I'll show, the
    formal mechanisms
of suspense perceived before and after in motion
become an index of the somatic tolls of risk; the visual
    excesses that we say

of gore that time has are now the signs elapsed
of financial contagion and toxicity. Like the guilt character-
    ization is like,
the moral thread of complex financial derivatives which,
as "Frankenstein's monsters" Raimi's film draws on, dupli-
    cates

the traditions of horror, the thread of time.
To describe, I once heard a new kind of terror—
a learned man—say
the deadliness of financialized debt and credit crisis.

That in offering a surprisingly nuanced representation is
    nothing
but of the contemporary financial economy, *Drag Me to
    Hell.*
The movement of the sun and the moon and the stars
also allows us to track larger historical transformations in
    both markets and culture.

I want to make two related arguments concerning these
   changes.
But I did not agree. First, unlike eighteenth-century novels
   of credit,
but we apprehend time only when we have marked mo-
   tion, marking it by early-twentieth-century financial
   panic novels, and a long tradition of horror-
   genre economic allegories,
Drag Me to Hell refuses either before or after

to contain economic anxiety or to imagine a restored calcu-
   lus for accountability.
And it is only when we have perceived before and after.
   Second, I see this refusal
in motion as a consequence of a fundamental shift in the
   relationship between credit and financial markets.
That we say. That time, particularly the introduction of
   commodified risk into the credit transaction, has
   elapsed.[x]

Act Three: Scene Three

P, Q, and R are in a parlor distinguished by staggered gradients of monochromatic white light in identically wide rays, in imitation of certain sequences of Jonathan Demme's film Stop Making Sense. *They await the appearance of S, to whom the parlor belongs, in imitation of Djuna Barnes'* Three from the Earth. *The space of action is blocked by linens as in the opening scene, indicating that this is S's space. If her visitors appear ill at ease, it is for a combination of reasons. First, they are aware of the indelicate imitations they are being forced to enact. (They slavishly remake Barnes' play.) Second, the air here is thick and unsatisfying, perhaps toxic. Of course S is immune.*

R.
Oh what luck to be the spawn of father's mistress—and to bury their letters—

(S enters.)

P.
Civics lesson! Earth is family resemblance. The enchantment thereof—

S.
Thank you.

Q.
As you please—

S.
—don't sound so significant. In country folk it equals hostility…

Q.
…to city folk it must seem so.

S.
Or dream, depending. Anyway, there'll be no taking credit for my hospitality, boys. You're here now. This is what you've come for. *(She becomes uncharacteristically animated, taking on the airs of a host, with disingenuous detail to gesture and expression.)* After all day fetching supper, I hardly have the strength to enjoy it. One can only sleep all night.

P.
Who knew you were so... *(looking for the word)*

S.
...dimensionless...

P.
...that you'd have room to harbor the patriarch...

S.
(correction)...alphabet.

P.
—the alphabet.

Q.
Despite the scenery, the country consists in solely genetic functions—just self-satisfying processes—indifference and plenitude.

R.
We knew no turmoil, no profit from misfortune, only knowledge to reflect the matters at hand.

P.
Shit.

R.
What?

Q.
He said…

P.
The *shit* is scenic. Everything counts. Nothing fails to matter. The explitive is only appropriate.

R.
Exactly…You get intruders, typical moralists, typical absolutes: socialists and cross-bearers, a veritable population at points.

P.
Hobbling on four corners, getting into everything.

Q.
But you can't complain.

R.
We're too untrained to make demands.

S.
(Derisive laughter.) John, you're waxing!

R.
Yes! An absence of all malfeasance.

P.
Father used to say if you can't spell it, don't speak it.

R.
And he never once spoke of…

S.
Your father could go from sleazy to saccharine in a single key stroke.

Q.
You misspelled saccharine.

P.
He did.

R.
He never did talk about you.

S.
He'd have needed an interpreter—a translator.

R.
Hoary wellwishes, carnal, putrid, and back again at a glance.

S.
My face.

R.
Your fuselage.

S.
Visage...rather do you mean...

Q.
Spell that.

P.
shit...

S.
…what? What is it?

P.
Your subways smell like piss.

S.
Your complaints reek, by the way.

P.
The escalators slurp as they unravel, and the ceilings drool.

S.
A list of spittle, listing.

R.
Father's silence was antiseptic. Without it, slapstick.

S.
Scatological slapstick, I'm afraid…peaty fields and banks of ponds floating lilies, what-not.

R.
…something nice and secluded…

Q.
…from mannerism, taste, or sobriety.

R.
Where we could be alone, breathing the same air. *(Takes S's hand to kiss it.)* But father couldn't stand seclusion. He excluded you. Fecundity threatened virility.

S. *(Removing her hand from R's.)*
Not that old sickly passionate in the way of resenting—You con-

sider me an epistemological tart only because it behooves you to believe in the lowest of the good. But those same sainted lips that kiss could cackle at diaper mishaps, shenanigans at the dinner table, what not—so you need it to behoove him to love evil—since to conceive and bear something is to obligate love, and evil is the concept adequate to resentment. Like seasons, years, generations align with the acknowledged grace of an unknown heteronymous series, there is failure, then obedience, finally meat. What does it take to turn to meat? Husbandry, you think, and you'd be right. But what follows from that? In the glow of your moodlit jukebox, nothing agreeable, I'm afraid. The point: address the melody to relevant findings. "Johnny B. Goode" is a family saga without the dirty little secret. A locomotive prosody fit for electro-prosthetic plainsong is just one reading. Another is celebrity, simple absolution, the elegance of a default incompatibility with failure. We should be equally shameless, not more or less to blame. Why should the matriarch not inaugurate, even foretell, this most American of celebrations?

R.
I can see it now: http://womenlaughingwithsalad.tumblr.com/

S.
(To R and by extension the rest.) You were cursed from birth.

P.
What does that make you?

R.
Reincarnated?

Q.
Spell that!

NOTES

[i] Some consider these Emily Dickinson's last words.

[ii] Mash up of Wallace Fowlie's translation of Arthur Rimbaud's "Bateau Ivre" and "U.S. Dollar Hegemony Has Got to Go" by Henry C K Liu, *Asia Times Online*, April 11, 2002.

[iii] S is quoting John Dewey's *Art as Experience*.

[iv] *Plaisir d'amour en Iran* (1976).

[v] *Frau X* (1934).

[vi] Une Forme
Pour désenchaîner l'Art du bavardage
l'Inititation des bondieuseries
Les Organismes de la corruption
Le Pouvoir de la bêtise
La Richesse de la laideur

Q cites a few lines from Werewere Liking's "chant-roman" *It Shall Be of Jasper and Coral,* trans. by Seanna Sumalee Oakley, in *Common Places: The Poetics of African Atlantic Postromantics,* Amsterdam: Rodopi, 2011.

[vii] That last line is from an internal questionnaire of the Art & Language group (1975).

[viii] R is quoting Robert Musil.

[ix] "Nobody has met any one." Stein, *Listen to Me* (1936).

[x] Mash up of the introductory paragraphs of Annie McClanahan's "Dead Pledges: Debt, Horror, and the Credit Crisis" (*Post 45,* 5/7/2012, http://post45.research.yale.edu/archives/2291) with the following passages:

"I once heard a learned man say that time is nothing but the movement of the sun and the moon and the stars, but I did not agree."—Saint Augustine, *Confessions*, XI, 23:29.

"But we apprehend time only when we have marked motion, marking it by before and after; and it is only when we have perceived before and after in motion that we say that time has elapsed."—Aristotle, *Physics*, IV, 220a.

"Guilt is like the moral thread which duplicates the thread of time."—Deleuze, "Four Poetic Formulas which Might Summarize the Kantian Philosophy."

ACKNOWLEDGMENTS

PQRS combines material either published or in notebooks dating back to the late 1990s with texts composed in the weeks leading up to the printing of this book. In the case of previously published text, it has been altered significantly in the process. This and my generally poor memory make accurate acknowledgements difficult, probably impossible. "The hand that slants" appeared in *Imitation Poems* (Atticus/Finch) and Q's soliloquy in 1:3 derives from a poem I discussed in a piece for *WIG*, while the poem appeared in an early form in *Mark(s)zine*. One of the series of *Imitation Poems* published in *Dusie* and read for *Weird Deer* left traces here as well. *Rabbit Light Movies* and *West Wind Review* featured "Untitled (fiat currency)," which Q recites in 1:1. 2:2 was informed by the suggestions of several friends: Jesse Seldess, Kevin Killian, Devin King, Rodney Koeneke, Laura Elrick, Tyrone

Williams, Pamela Lu, and (obviously) Tan Lin. Special thanks to them, and especially to Tyrone for agreeing to feature his poem. Participating in productions of work by Carla Harryman, Laynie Browne, Bill Luoma, and K. Silem Mohammad inspired me to enter the field of poets theater. Working with Killian and David Brazil on *The Kenning Anthology of Poets Theater*, and later teaching from that book, ultimately convinced me to finish this work. I admire these people greatly. Thanks to all.

I have read from *PQRS* for Series A in Chicago, Big Night in Buffalo, NY, and Felix in Madison, WI. Some of this you can hear at *Penn Sound*.

KENNING EDITIONS

Waveform, by Amber DiPietra and Denise Leto. ISBN: 978-0-9767364-9-3 $10.00

Propagation, by Laura Elrick. ISBN: 978-0-9846475-8-3 $14.95

The Kenning Anthology of Poets Theater: 1945-1985, edited by Kevin Killian and David Brazil. ISBN: 978-0-9767364-5-5 $25.95

Insomnia and the Aunt, by Tan Lin. ISBN: 978-0-9767364-7-9 $13.95

Ambient Parking Lot, by Pamela Lu. ISBN: 978-0-9767364-3-1 $14.95

Some Math, by Bill Luoma. ISBN: 978-0-9767364-6-2 $14.95

The Pink, by Kyle Schlesinger. ISBN: 978-0-9767364-4-8 $7.50

Who Opens, by Jesse Seldess. ISBN: 978-0-9767364-0-0 $12.95

Left Having, by Jesse Seldess. ISBN: 978-0-9767364-8-6 $14.95

Hannah Weiner's Open House, by Hannah Weiner, edited and with an introduction by Patrick F. Durgin. ISBN: 978-0-9767364-1-7 $14.95

Kenning Editions are distributed to individuals and the trade by Small Press Distribution. See spdbooks.org

For updates, orders and events, see kenningeditions.com